SOUTHERN
STEAM
IN RETROSPECT

ERIC SAWFORD

SUTTON PUBLISHING

First published in 2007 by
Sutton Publishing Limited · Phoenix Mill
Thrupp · Stroud · Gloucestershire · GL5 2BU

British Library Cataloguing in Publication Data
A catalogue record for this book is available from the British Library.

ISBN 978-0-7509-4627-8

Front endpaper: E1. no. 32113 shunting wagons at Southampton Docks. In total, seventy-nine E1s were built between 1874 and 1891 and most enjoyed a long working life. The first was withdrawn in 1908 and the last in 1961.   9.11.55

Back endpaper: Merchant Navy class no. 35004 *Cunard White Star* at its home shed, Exmouth Junction. Completed at Eastleigh in October 1941, it was rebuilt in July 1958 and remained in service until October 1965.   3.9.56

Title page photograph: West Country class no. 34098 *Templecombe* waits to return to its home depot, Ramsgate, following a general overhaul at Eastleigh works. This engine was rebuilt in February 1961 and withdrawn in June 1967.   9.11.55

Typeset in 10/12pt Palatino.
Typesetting and origination by
Sutton Publishing Limited.
Printed and bound in England.

Contents

El no. 32113 at Southampton Docks.

C14 0-4-0T no. 30588 at Southampton West Quay.

Introduction

In 1948, following nationalisation, each of the six British Railway regions still had very interesting veteran locomotives hard at work. In many cases the longevity of such engines resulted from special requirements. The Southern Region was no exception, having two branches where the locomotives had long outlived their classmates; both of these were in the West Country and became a great attraction for enthusiasts and tourists alike.

During the 1950s many delightful country branches were still in operation, and one of these was the Axminster to Lyme Regis line. For much of the year traffic was steady, but this changed in the summer months as at this time many holidaymakers still travelled by rail. Motive power for the branch was two, later three, elegant 4–4–2Ts, nos 30582–4. An Adams design dating back to 1882, these radial tank engines were widely used on suburban and branch line services. In all seventy-one were built between 1882 and 1885 by four different private companies. They were first introduced to the Lyme Regis branch in 1913, but it was found that they needed greater side play on the bogies in order to cope with the severe curves on the branch; this work was carried out at Eastleigh works. Two engines were duly modified, and their return to Lyme Regis marked the start of a long association with the branch. They worked there for forty-eight years, apart from a short period in the late 1920s when they required heavy repairs and a decision was made to trial other classes, none of which proved successful. As a result the two Adams engines were given major overhauls and returned to the branch.

The remainder of the class were withdrawn in 1928, leaving just the two 4–4–2Ts handling services on the branch until after the Second World War. One member of the class had been sold to the Ministry of Munitions during the First World War and had ended up on the East Kent Railway, where it was lying derelict by the 1940s. The Southern Railway decided to make an approach regarding its purchase. On inspection, it was found to require a new firebox, but despite this and the ravages of the weather it was deemed repairable, and was duly purchased for £800. It was transported to Eastleigh works where it received a general overhaul. It was then officially taken into Southern Railway stock and dispatched in December 1946 to the West Country. In due course all three engines were in fully serviceable condition, although only one engine was normally required on the branch for most of the year. The other two were employed on various duties around Exeter. The first of the trio was withdrawn in January 1961, and the other two were condemned later in the year. Fortunately, no. 30583, the engine that was originally bought from the East Kent Railway, gained a new lease of life when it was purchased by the Bluebell Railway.

Without doubt, in the 1950s the Southern Region's biggest attraction for enthusiasts was to be found at the Cornish town of Wadebridge. The railwaymen there were already very familiar with the stream of enthusiasts attracted by the three veteran 2–4–0 Beattie 'well tanks', which had long outlived their classmates. Introduced in 1874, with twelve examples built in 1874–5, these three unique well tanks had managed to survive owing to the fact that they were ideally suited for use on the Wenford Bridge mineral line transporting china clay. During their working lives they had been rebuilt by three successive Locomotive Superintendents, W. Adams, R.W. Urie and, in Southern Railway days, R.E.L. Maunsell. In 1888 the first of the class was condemned after a comparatively short working life, and by the time of the Grouping in 1923 only the three used on the Wenford Bridge branch

Countless enthusiasts, myself included, alighted at Axminster to catch the branch line service to the very attractive seaside resort of Lyme Regis. During the 1950s the rail services were in the hands of the veteran Adams 4–4–2Ts. For most of the year only one engine was required, but in the summer months, especially at weekends, all three examples were required to cope with the volume of holidaymakers who, at that time, still mostly travelled by rail. No. 30582 is seen here backing on to the branch train at Axminster.   3.9.56

remained. The last of these was withdrawn from service in 1962, and happily two of them have survived into preservation.

In the 1950s the Southern was a region of contrasts. Electric trains provided many services, alongside the Bulleid Pacifics working the main line to the West Country and (prior to electrification) the Kent coast services. One of their duties was the prestigious 'Golden Arrow' service from Victoria to Folkestone, one of the many services connecting with the Channel ferries. In contrast, the Southern also had a considerable number of veteran and other interesting locomotives still in service, in addition to those already mentioned.

In November 1955 I made a photographic trip to Southampton, and my first call was Eastleigh locomotive depot. This was a very interesting shed with a wide range of types to be seen, including Pacifics either awaiting works or fresh from general overhaul. Many other classes were also maintained by Eastleigh, including the N15 King Arthur class 4–6–0s, a design first introduced by R.W. Urie for the London & South Western Railway in 1918. In all, seventy-four were built, and all were named. The N15X Remembrance class, also 4–6–0s, consisted of just seven locomotives, and here again all named. In some ways these rebuilt engines resembled the King Arthur class but they were from a very different origin, beginning life as London, Brighton & South Coast Railway 4–6–4Ts introduced by L.B. Billinton in 1914. They were rebuilt under the direction of R.E.L. Maunsell from 1934. The seven locomotives of this class were all allocated to Basingstoke shed, where their main duties were local services to Waterloo. The first engine was withdrawn in 1955, with the last going two years later.

The principal express passenger locomotives of the Southern Region introduced in 1941 were the Merchant Navy class, consisting of thirty locomotives. Nine Elms had the largest number, with others allocated to Salisbury and Exmouth Junction and a further four at Stewarts Lane. These engines were principally used for working boat trains, among them

In the 1950s E4 0–6–2Ts were to be found at many depots as there were seventy in service, plus four rebuilt to E4X. Nine Elms had several in its allocation, including no. 32476. The design was introduced by L.B. Billinton for the LBSCR in 1910, a development of the E3 class which made its debut in 1894. The E4s had smaller driving wheels. 14.7.54

Tender locomotives of the 0–6–0 wheel arrangement were commonplace on all regions, although the smallest number were to be found on the Western Region. C class no. 31510, a visitor from Gillingham, is seen here at Hither Green. Fourteen examples were allocated to this depot. 24.5.56

the 'Golden Arrow' and the 'Night Ferry'. Two more Merchant Navy class engines were allocated to Dover shed, but their appearance was considerably changed on rebuilding.

In 1945 O.V. Bulleid introduced a new type of lightweight Pacific in the form of the West Country and Battle of Britain classes, again with air-smoothed casing. Apart from their names, the two classes were identical. Unlike the Merchant Navy class engines, which were all rebuilt, a number of these lightweight 4–6–2 Pacifics ended their days in un-rebuilt form. Prior to electrification they were also widely used on Kent coast services, as well as services to and in the West Country. Brighton depot had five in its allocation, principally working services to Salisbury. Sizeable allocations of these engines were also to be found at several other sheds, including Nine Elms, Bournemouth, Exmouth Junction, Salisbury and Plymouth Friary.

Prior to the introduction of the Bulleid Pacifics the most powerful Southern Railway express locomotives were the sixteen Lord Nelson class 4–6–0s introduced in 1926. Initially problems were experienced with these engines, but in their later years they were considerably improved, becoming generally trouble-free in service when fitted with Lemaitre multiple-jet blastpipes. In the 1950s many of the express services were in the hands of Pacifics but the Lord Nelsons still provided invaluable service and were often to be seen hauling the Southampton boat trains. In the mid-1950s Nine Elms depot had three of these engines in its allocation, with other members of the class to be found at Eastleigh and Bournemouth. Withdrawals commenced in 1961, the last going in the following year. Fortunately, one, no. 30850 *Lord Nelson*, has survived into preservation.

Maunsell introduced a number of new classes during his term in office. Without doubt, his finest passenger design was the Schools class 4–4–0s. These three-cylinder engines were officially classified V class and made their debut in 1930. Forty engines were built, all at Eastleigh works. The entire class was named after public and private boarding schools. The Southern Region was certainly not lacking in publicity skills, and wherever possible the new locomotives were taken to the station nearest the school it was named after and placed on exhibition to the pupils. This doubtless fostered a great deal of interest in pupils and enthusiasts alike, especially in areas where the class was not generally seen. The Schools were regarded as the finest 4–4–0s to run in Britain, and they were very popular with enginemen for their excellent capabilities and handling. From 1938 a number were fitted with multiple-jet blastpipes and a large chimney, and this altered their appearance considerably. In the early 1950s the largest allocation of these engines was to be found at Bricklayers Arms, with others at Ramsgate, Dover and St Leonards. The class was considerably affected by the south-east section electrification, and following this they became more familiar in other areas. Withdrawals commenced in 1961, and the last members of the class were withdrawn in the following year. Three were preserved, including no. 30925 *Cheltenham*.

The Southern Region relied heavily on locomotives with the 4–4–0 wheel arrangement. I found the examples built by the London & South Western Railway particularly interesting. On my first visit to Nine Elms in July 1951 I discovered L11 class no. 30163, built at Nine Elms works in 1903, standing in the yard. It was in the depot's allocation at the time and was principally used on parcel and empty stock duties, running with an eight-wheel tender, but time was already running out for this veteran engine as it was withdrawn in the following October. The L11 and the very similar but slightly smaller K10s were graceful designs, easily recognised by their distinctive tall chimneys. Sadly both these classes became extinct in 1951.

Three other 4–4–0 ex-LSWR types, again with a distinctive outline, were the S11, L12 and D15 classes. These were principal express locomotives in their day. By the 1950s, however, they were employed on secondary services, parcels and empty stock workings. The majority of the S11s were withdrawn in 1951, leaving just one to soldier on until 1954. Similarly, all except one of the L12s were withdrawn in 1951; the exception, based at Guildford, made it to 1955. The ten D15s were all built at Eastleigh works in 1912. In their final years two were to be found at Nine Elms. In July 1954 I found no. 30467 standing

Two M7 0–4–4Ts, no. 30039 and no. 30035, pictured at Clapham Junction. At the time other M7s were also working on empty stock duties. Both of these engines spent a considerable time in the West Country, and both ended their days on this work. Both completed a very commendable sixty-five years' service.   9.61

One of the Tonbridge shed fitters carries out a visual examination of H class 0–4–4T no. 31276. Over fifty examples, including this one, were equipped for push-pull working.   1.7.53

The O1 class consisted of fifty-eight rebuilds by Wainwright of the Stirling O class design introduced in 1878. Not all were rebuilt – the original O class was 122-strong. Rebuilding included a domed boiler and new cab. Here, no. 31064 is seen at Ashford shunting engineers' wagons. These engines were easily recognised by the external tender frames and springs.   1.7.53

alone in a splendid position in the yard, making it ideal for photography. The D15s had large-diameter boilers and were powerful free-running engines that were highly regarded by enginemen. The last example was withdrawn in 1956.

The most numerous of the LSWR 4–4–0s were the T9s, often referred to as 'Greyhounds'. These engines, with their 6ft 7in driving wheels, were certainly capable of a fair turn of speed, hence their nickname. Introduced in 1899 to the design of Dugald Drummond, they were built by Dubs & Co. and also at Nine Elms works. The last example from the latter was completed in 1901. During the 1950s these locomotives were widely used on cross-country services in the West Country and many will have fond memories of their work on the long-closed Padstow branch.

Several of the South Eastern & Chatham Railway 4–4–0s were still active in the early 1950s, although by this time the graceful D class locomotives introduced by Wainwright in 1901 were steadily being withdrawn. These engines had a distinctive round-topped firebox, and they were built at several locations including Ashford works, as well as by four private companies, Dubs & Co., Sharp, Stewart & Co., R. Stephenson & Co. and the Vulcan Foundry. Construction took place over a three-year period. In 1921 Maunsell decided to rebuild a number of these engines with superheated Belpaire boilers and long-travel piston valves. These rebuilt locomotives, classified D1, were very different in appearance.

In 1905 Wainwright introduced another 4–4–0 design, this time with a Belpaire boiler. Thirteen were built at Ashford between 1906 and 1908. In 1920 five were rebuilt with larger superheated boilers and long-travel piston valves, and these became class E1. The last of the un-rebuilt engines was withdrawn in 1954.

Just before the First World War the final Wainwright 4–4–0 design was introduced. The class L engines had detail alteration by Maunsell, who had taken over as Locomotive Superintendent on the SECR. In all twenty-two were built, twelve by Beyer, Peacock & Co. and the remaining ten by A. Borsig of Germany. In 1926 the first of the fifteen class L1s was

Having worked in with the famous 'Golden Arrow' Pullman service, Merchant Navy class no. 35026 *Lamport & Holt Line* proceeds to the small locomotive depot for servicing and turning ready for the return journey. This engine ended its days at Weymouth shed, from where it was withdrawn in March 1967. 5.7.53

Schools class no. 30913 *Christ's Hospital* of Ramsgate shed arrives at Clapham Junction station. Introduced by Maunsell in 1930, the class continued to be constructed at Eastleigh works until 1935. Two were withdrawn in 1961, with the rest of the forty-strong class going the following year. 9.61

A splendid line-up pictured at Stewarts Lane. On the left is King Arthur class no. 30763 *Sir Bors de Ganis*, alongside D1 no. 31487, and on the right is E1 no. 31067. In the early 1950s all three of these classes were frequently seen on express passenger services.   1.11.51

introduced, the L1s being a post-Grouping development. Among the modifications were slide-window cabs, long-travel valves and other detail alterations. During the early 1950s both classes could be seen on the south-eastern section carrying out a variety of duties.

Being fortunate enough to remember the Great Northern's Atlantics I was keen to capture on film at least one of the famous Brighton Atlantics. The first class designed by Marsh for the London, Brighton & South Coast Railway, the H1 class locomotives became extinct in 1951, while the later H2 class, introduced in 1911, still had five in service in the early 1950s, one having been withdrawn in 1949. They were allocated to Brighton, where their duties included the Newhaven boat trains. Four were withdrawn in 1956, leaving just no. 32424 *Beachy Head*, which remained in service until 1958. This was to be the last Atlantic to run in normal revenue service.

As with other regions, the Southern also had a sizeable stud of mixed traffic locomotives, including the H15 class 4–6–0s that boasted considerable variation. The most numerous mixed traffic engines were the N class 2–6–0s introduced by Maunsell in 1917 for the South Eastern & Chatham Railway. In 1922 a three-cylinder development was introduced; in all six locomotives were built and became class N1. In 1928 Maunsell, who by then was Locomotive Superintendent of the Southern Railway, commenced rebuilding the unsuccessful K class 2–6–4Ts known as the River class; in rebuilt form these became class U 2–6–0s. Some new locomotives were also constructed and, as with the N class, a three-cylinder development followed. Twenty-one U1s were constructed from 1928 onwards. These 2–6–0 designs were invaluable and could be found working throughout the region on both passenger and freight workings. There was also a class of seventeen 2–6–0s originating from the London, Brighton & South Coast Railway. Introduced in 1913, they became the K class.

The S15 4–6–0s classified 6F were introduced in 1920 to the design of Robert Urie for the London & South Western Railway. These were a development of the King Arthur class but

In the early 1950s all ten examples of the E1R class 0–6–2Ts were to be found at depots within the Exmouth Junction district. Some were used on branch line duties, while those based at Exmouth Junction were principally employed on banking duties at Exeter and shunting work. No. 32697 was photographed at work near the depot.   3.9.56

with 5ft 7in driving wheels as opposed to the 6ft 7in wheels of the original passenger locomotives. A considerable number of S15s were allocated to Feltham, a depot serving one of the principal goods yards. In all, there were forty-five locomotives in the class.

One wheel arrangement that was invaluable on all regions was the 0–6–0, and such engines numbered among their duties passenger services, goods workings and pick-up freights. The most modern examples on the Southern Region were the forty Bulleid Austerity Q1 class engines which caused a considerable stir when they were introduced in 1942 owing to their unconventional design. Four years earlier Maunsell had introduced the Q class; twenty were built at Eastleigh works and all remained in service until the early 1960s. In later years these engines were easily recognisable when fitted with Lemaitre blastpipes and large-diameter chimneys. Other 0–6–0 designs included the C class, introduced by Wainwright for the South Eastern & Chatham Railway. There were more than a hundred of these in service in the early 1950s. The 01 class consisted of rebuilds by Wainwright of an 1878 design, these veterans being easily recognisable by their outside frames and springs on the tender. The London & South Western Railway operated thirty 0–6–0s of the 700 class; all remained active in the early 1950s, with the first being withdrawn in 1957. The others survived until the early 1960s. Feltham depot also had several of the remaining 0395 class 0–6–0s in its allocation; these were principally used on local goods workings and shunting in the area. Adams had introduced this 1881 design, and considerable variations were to be found among them.

The Southern Region had a wide range of tank locomotives, some of which have already been mentioned. I just had to visit Feltham depot, which was concerned with freight workings so the only passenger locomotives to be found there were visitors. The biggest attractions at Feltham were the two classes of large tank locomotives allocated there, in both cases consisting of the entire class. The four massive G16 4–8–0Ts were introduced by Urie in 1921 for 'hump shunting' in the marshalling yards. When not engaged on this work they were also used on goods workings in the London area. Two were withdrawn in 1959, and the other two went into store. The second class of large tanks comprised the five H16 4–6–2Ts, nos 30516–20. Also introduced in 1921, they were used on interchange freight workings to the London Midland Region and local goods traffic. In the early 1960s some members of the class enjoyed a brief swansong on the Fawley branch oil trains but all five were withdrawn in 1962. These were not the only heavy tank engines to be found on the Southern Region. There was also a third class of eight heavy tank locomotives introduced in 1929 to the design of Maunsell and constructed at Brighton works. These were classified as Z class and in their latter years those employed on banking duties at Exeter were the best known. In 1962 several classes became extinct on the Southern, including all eight Zs, which were withdrawn over a three-month period.

To obtain photographs of the smaller classes it was usually necessary to visit a depot to give yourself the best chance of finding what you wanted. This was certainly the case with the W class 2–6–4Ts. Hither Green had more than half of the total class in its allocation, their principal duties being inter-regional freight workings. These engines were a development of the N class 2–6–0s introduced by Maunsell in 1931, and in all fifteen were built.

In 1946 the Southern Region decided to purchase fourteen of the surplus US Army Transportation 0–6–0Ts. These were thoroughly overhauled, receiving modified cabs, bunkers and other details, before being sent to Southampton Docks where, in the early 1950s, they worked alongside several E1 0–6–0Ts. The small shed (code 71I) was in what was known as the Eastern Docks, but it lost its steam allocation in June 1963, diesel shunters having already taken over many of the duties.

With numerous branch lines still in operation in the 1950s a considerable number of small tank engines were to be seen throughout the Southern Region. These ranged from the H class 0–4–4Ts of the eastern section to the well-known M7 0–4–4Ts which also worked empty stock in and out of Waterloo. There were also several other classes to be found in ever-decreasing numbers, such as the G6 0–6–0Ts of LSWR origin, the tiny P class 0–6–0Ts originally designed for push-pull working and the D3 0–4–4Ts of London, Brighton & South Coast Railway origin, again principally designed for push-pull working. There were several classes within the E prefix, consisting of a mixture of 0–6–0T and 0–6–2T designs. Great favourites with enthusiasts were the Terriers, which had their swan song on the Hayling Island branch. Even more unusual were the three C14 0–4–0Ts, two of which were used on shunting work at Southampton West Quay. The third, DS77, was photographed at Brighton works in LBSR livery. These were rebuilds of 2–2–0T rail motors introduced in 1906.

One tank class that should certainly not be overlooked was the 02 0–4–4Ts introduced by Adams for the LSWR in 1889. A considerable number were to be found at work on the mainland, with twenty-three on the Isle of Wight, together with four E1 0–6–0Ts. There were two depots on the island, at Ryde and Newport, the former operating all 02s fitted with Westinghouse brake and enlarged bunkers. In 1957 Newport shed closed and the remaining engines were transferred to Ryde, which itself finished with steam in March 1967, the reduced island line having been electrified.

During the early and mid-1950s the Somerset & Dorset line was part of the Southern Region. It had locomotive depots at Bath (Green Park) allocated 71G, Templecombe (71H) and the small shed at Highbridge (71J). In 1958 the S&D was taken over by the Western Region before closure in March 1966. One class of locomotives well known for their work on the S&D were the eleven 7F 2–8–0s, a Fowler design first introduced in 1914. These were all allocated to Bath (Green Park). Overhauls of these engines continued to be carried out at Derby works, despite the fact they came under the jurisdiction of the Southern Region. Other former LMS classes were also allocated to the S&D depots, along with a few locomotives of the British Railways Standard designs. In retrospect, in the 1950s the Southern had much to offer the enthusiast. Despite the large areas already electrified, there were many veteran locomotives still hard at work, with the famous Bulleid Pacifics in charge of some passenger services until the region finished with steam in July 1967.

Chapter One
Tender Locomotives

The appointment of Oliver Bulleid to the position of Chief Mechanical Engineer for the Southern Railway in 1937 resulted in dramatic changes to the rather desperate motive power situation, which had been short of the funding required for new steam locomotives. Electrification of the lines had taken priority, in turn resulting in increased fare receipts. Bulleid, however, soon brought steam back to the fore.

In 1941 the first Merchant Navy class Pacific emerged from Eastleigh works, with air-smoothed casing that was very different from conventional locomotives. The appearance of these engines during war time was unusual in itself. Thirty were built at Eastleigh between 1941 and 1949, and all were named after famous shipping lines. In 1945 the first of Bulleid's West Country lightweight Pacifics emerged from Brighton works. In total, 110 were built between 1945 and 1951, mostly at Brighton works, although six were produced at Eastleigh. Included in this total were a number of engines known as the Battle of Britain class, which were identical in every way except for their names. Many of these engines were to be found in the West Country, at Nine Elms and also in other parts of the Southern Region. Rebuilding of the Merchant Navy class commenced in 1956 and continued through until 1959. The last two were modified and returned to traffic in October 1959. Similar treatment was also given to a number of the lightweight Pacifics, while others continued in un-rebuilt form right through to withdrawal.

The Maunsell-designed passenger locomotives were still active in the 1950s, although some of the King Arthurs were already being relegated to secondary duties. With the electrification of the eastern section, many engines were made redundant. Withdrawals of the West Country/Battle of Britain locomotives commenced in 1963 with the un-rebuilt examples. The following year was to see the first of the Merchant Navy class withdrawn.

In the early 1950s the Southern Region relied heavily on various 4–4–0s, many of which were pre-Grouping locomotives. There was also the powerful Maunsell Schools class introduced in 1930. By this time withdrawals were steadily taking place of the pre-Grouping engines, although some designs, the T9s among them, were still widely used on cross-country and secondary routes together with parcel trains.

Each of the regions operated six-coupled locomotives on freight duties, but none was as unconventional as the Q1 class 0–6–0s on the Southern, again introduced by Bulleid, in this case in 1942. These were Austerity engines and their stark appearance certainly caused considerable comment when they made their debut. In the early 1950s there were also a considerable number of veteran 0–6–0s still in service, including the South Eastern Railway's 01s with their outside tender frames and the 0395 class, an LSWR design dating back to 1881. Several of the latter were allocated to Feltham depot and could be seen shunting in the London suburbs. In contrast the 700 class engines introduced in 1897, despite their age, had a much more modern appearance. There were other classes too, the last to appear before the war being the Maunsell Qs introduced in 1938.

One famous class that was active up to the mid-1950s comprised the Brighton Atlantics, still used on the Newhaven boat trains. On the two occasions that I visited Brighton shed two or three were present, but their days were numbered.

It was not until 1959 that the last of the Merchant Navy class engines were rebuilt. No. 35004 *Cunard White Star*, seen here at its home shed, Exmouth Junction, was completed at Eastleigh in October 1941 and made its debut as no. 21C4, receiving its BR number in April 1948. Rebuilt in July 1958, it remained in service until October 1965. After a few months in store at Eastleigh works it was scrapped in February 1966.   3.9.56

The prestigious 'Golden Arrow' service, headed by Merchant Navy class no. 35026 *Lamport & Holt Line*, arrives at Folkestone Junction station. A few minutes later the engine would hand over to an R1 class 0–6–0T, which would work the train down to the harbour station to connect with the cross-channel ferry.   5.7.53

In immaculate condition Merchant Navy no. 35026 *Lamport & Holt Line*, complete with the 'Golden Arrow' insignia and British and French flags, stands on the turntable at Folkestone Junction shed. No. 35026 was completed at Eastleigh in December 1948, rebuilt in January 1957 and withdrawn in March 1967.   5.7.53

Another view of Merchant Navy no. 35026 *Lamport & Holt Line*, one of Stewarts Lane depot's top link engines. It was certainly no stranger to Folkestone and Dover. When this photograph was taken at Folkestone Junction shed it had worked in with a boat train and was in the process of being turned.   3.7.53

A platelayer watches as Merchant Navy class no. 35026 *Lamport & Holt Line* speeds through Folkestone Junction at the head of the 'Night Ferry' London–Paris service via Dover. This engine was one of four allocated to Stewarts Lane depot. During one week I photographed this engine on three separate occasions, heading the 'Night Ferry', the 'Golden Arrow' and a connecting boat train.   5.7.53

(*Opposite, top*): Resplendent in blue livery at Nine Elms, this is Merchant Navy no. 35015 *Rotterdam Lloyd*. Repainted in June 1953 in Brunswick green, it was rebuilt five years later and transferred to Nine Elms, where it ended its service life in February 1964.   5.7.51

(*Opposite, bottom*): Having worked in to Waterloo with an express from the West Country, Merchant Navy no. 35022 *Holland–America Line* waits for the signal to proceed to Nine Elms for servicing. Completed in October 1948, this engine was rebuilt in June 1956 and withdrawn just under ten years later.   7.7.51

Merchant Navy class no. 35015 *Rotterdam Lloyd* and no. 35014 *Nederland Line* pictured in immaculate condition at Nine Elms, their home depot. Completed in 1945, they were rebuilt in 1958 and 1956 respectively. No. 35015 was withdrawn from service in February 1964, while no. 35014 soldiered on until March 1967.   5.7.51

Merchant Navy no. 35011 *General Steam Navigation*, seen here taking water at Nine Elms, was still in malachite green livery with its tender lettered British Railways when this photograph was taken. It was repainted in Brunswick green at the end of that year. It was rebuilt in July 1959 and withdrawn in February 1966.   5.7.51

Merchant Navy class no. 35019 *French Line CGT* passes through Clapham Junction on its way to Waterloo. The entire class of thirty locomotives was rebuilt between 1956 and 1959, and some remained in service on the Southern Region right to the end of steam in July 1967. 9.61

Only a few months after being rebuilt at Eastleigh works, Merchant Navy class no. 35020 *Bibby Line* awaits the 'right away' from Waterloo with the 'Atlantic Coast Express'. This engine was completed in June 1945 and withdrawn in February 1965. 3.9.56

Merchant Navy class no. 35007 *Aberdeen Commonwealth* pictured in good external condition at its home shed, Weymouth. It later moved to Nine Elms, where it remained in service until the end of steam on the Southern Region in July 1967. After seven months in store it ended its days at Buttigeigs of Newport in April 1968.   26.3.66

(*Opposite, top*): During its first few years in service Merchant Navy no. 35026 *Lamport & Holt Line* worked on the eastern section hauling boat trains to Folkestone and Dover, but its final years were spent at Weymouth shed, where it is seen being turned. Note the tatty surrounds of the turntable well, which had certainly seen better days. This engine was cut up at Cashmores of Newport in September 1967.   15.9.66

(*Opposite, bottom*): At the time of my visit in October 1965 the locomotives stored at Barry were still generally in quite good condition, although the cab glass had been broken on Merchant Navy no. 35006 *Peninsular & Oriental S.N.Co.* Barry was to become the best known of all the locomotive scrapyards, and a considerable number of engines that ended up there were fortunate to survive into preservation, often being rescued in a terrible condition.   25.10.65

West Country class no. 34020 *Seaton* heads a London-bound express through Eastleigh station. This engine was completed in December 1945; it was not rebuilt and was withdrawn in September 1964.   9.11.55

(*Opposite, top*): Battle of Britain class no. 34078 *222 Squadron* passes Folkestone Central with a boat train relief. Completed in July 1948, this engine was never rebuilt and was withdrawn in September 1964.   28.6.53

(*Opposite, bottom*): Bulleid Pacifics either awaiting or fresh from a works visit were usually to be seen in the yards at Eastleigh. Here West Country no. 34098 *Templecombe* waits to return to its home depot, Ramsgate, following a general overhaul. This engine was rebuilt in February 1961 and withdrawn in June 1967.   9.11.55

Battle of Britain class no. 34061 *73 Squadron*, pictured at Waterloo. It was a Nine Elms engine at this time but it was later to spend several years at Exmouth Junction. Its final years were spent at a number of different sheds, but it was never rebuilt and was withdrawn in August 1964.   7.7.51

(*Opposite*): West Country class no. 34103 *Calstock* undergoing repairs in the yard at Ashford works. 'Not to be Moved' signs can be seen on both sides of the buffer beam, the engine presumably having failed en route. *Calstock* was a Stewarts Lane engine at the time. Built in 1950, it was never rebuilt and was withdrawn in September 1965.   1.7.53

Un-rebuilt Battle of Britain class no. 34086 *219 Squadron* in store at Weymouth. Almost certainly it never worked again, as it was withdrawn less than two months later. After four months in store at Eastleigh, it was sold for scrap to Buttigeigs of Newport.   23.3.66

In total, 110 West Country/Battle of Britain class Bulleid lightweight Pacifics were built. Of these, no fewer than fifty remained in un-rebuilt condition throughout their service life. No. 34023 *Blackmoor Vale* was completed at Brighton in February 1946, and remained in service until July 1967. It is seen here at Weymouth shed.   15.9.66

Battle of Britain class no. 34062 *17 Squadron*, pictured at Exmouth Junction shed in un-rebuilt form. This engine was rebuilt in April 1959 and remained in service until June 1964. It was an Exmouth Junction engine for many years and was still allocated there when it was withdrawn, the depot having by this time been taken over by the Western Region. It was dispatched to Birds of Bridgend and cut up there after standing for several months in their yard. 3.9.56

I photographed Battle of Britain class no. 34049 *Anti-Aircraft Command* in the yard of its home shed, Salisbury. Completed at Brighton works in December 1946 carrying the number 21C149, it did not receive its British Railways number until April 1949. It was not rebuilt and remained in service until December 1963, the year in which the first Bulleid lightweight Pacifics were withdrawn, ending its days at Eastleigh works in June 1964. 3.9.56

Twenty-four of the Battle of Britain class Bulleid Pacifics were named after Royal Air Force squadrons. No. 34078 *222 Squadron* is seen here at Bricklayers Arms. It was withdrawn from Exmouth Junction depot in September 1964 and two months later was sent to Birds of Morriston, Swansea, for scrapping.   1.11.51

Un-rebuilt West Country class no. 34092 *City of Wells* was withdrawn from Salisbury shed in December 1964. In March 1965, after a short period in store, it was moved to Barry, where this picture was taken. Several months later it was still very much in the condition in which it had arrived. Fortunately it was rescued for preservation and restored to working order. Originally named *Wells*, it became *City of Wells* in March 1950.   25.10.65

The Up 'Bournemouth Belle' approaches Brockenhurst headed by West Country class no. 34093 *Saunton*. Not only was the engine in poor external condition, typical of the period, but it had also lost its nameplates. Nevertheless it survived until the end of steam on the Southern Region in July 1967. 16.9.66

During the final years many of the Bulleid Pacifics ran without nameplates or front numberplates. No. 34060 *25 Squadron* is a typical example, with its number painted on the smokebox door but still carrying a 70D Basingstoke shedplate. This engine survived until the end of steam on the Southern Region four months later, ending its days at Cashmores of Newport.   12.3.67

Battle of Britain class no. 34071 *601 Squadron* in deplorable condition heads an Up empty stock working at Brockenhurst. This engine was rebuilt in May 1960. It appears that the inner panel of the nameplate had already been removed, and this engine's time in service was already running out as it was withdrawn in April 1967.   16.9.66

(*Opposite, top*): Rebuilt Battle of Britain class no. 34088 *213 Squadron* runs light engine through Clapham Junction station. At this time it was allocated to Nine Elms and may well have been on its way to Eastleigh works for attention.   9.61

(*Opposite, bottom*): Weymouth shed was just a shadow of its former self when this picture of Bulleid West Country class no. 34093 *Saunton* (minus nameplates) was taken. This engine was in service right up to the end of steam on the Southern. It spent seven months at Weymouth before being sent to Cashmores of Newport for scrapping.   26.3.66

During the 1950s the vast majority of the sixteen Lord Nelson class engines were allocated to Eastleigh and Bournemouth depots, with just three at Nine Elms. No. 30851 *Sir Francis Drake* had just returned to its home shed, Eastleigh. The first member of the class made its debut in 1926, but it was to be two years before production of the rest started. These engines were well liked and generally trouble-free in service. No. 30851 was withdrawn in December 1961 and cut up at Eastleigh works. 9.11.55

Several Lord Nelson class 4–6–0s were allocated to Bournemouth shed in the 1950s, no. 30861 *Lord Anson* among them. This engine had worked up to London with a morning service and arrived at Nine Elms for servicing; here the fire is in the process of being cleaned prior to coaling. Someone would have faced the unenviable task of removing all the ash and clinker seen in this picture. 24.5.56

Schools class no. 30932 *Blundells* of Bricklayers Arms depot awaits the 'right away' from Ramsgate with a London service. Note the array of station signs on the left: advertisements for Virol and Wright's soaps were once commonplace on many stations.   6.7.53

During the 1960s four examples of the Schools class were allocated to Nine Elms, no. 30906 *Sherborne* among them. It is seen here arriving at Clapham Junction as an express for Waterloo departs. The Schools locomotives were regarded as the best 4–4–0s to run on British metals.   9.61

Twenty examples of the Schools class were fitted with Lemaitre multiple-jet blastpipes and larger chimneys. No. 30907 *Dulwich*, seen here at Bricklayers Arms depot, was allocated to Ramsgate depot. Similar equipment was also fitted to engines in the Lord Nelson and King Arthur classes, and to the Q class 0–6–0s.   25.11.54

(*Opposite, top*): H15 class no. 30524 was one of the Maunsell locomotives with an N15-type boiler and a smaller tender. The BR number was carried on the smokebox and cabside but the word 'Southern' still appeared on the tender. At this time some engines were still lettered British Railways while others had received the BR crest.   5.7.51

(*Opposite, bottom*): At the time of my visit several King Arthur class engines were stored in the yard at Eastleigh shed. Among them was no. 30750 *Morgan le Fay*. This engine was one of the Urie locomotives introduced in 1928 and modified with cylinders of reduced diameter. Completed at Eastleigh in October 1922, it was withdrawn in July 1957.   8.11.55

Happily for me it was possible to take photographs in the part of Eastleigh shed where King Arthur class no. 30789 *Sir Guy* was under repair. This engine was one of the batch built for the eastern section in 1925 by the North British Company, with modified cabs and new bogie tenders.   8.11.55

Stewarts Lane depot King Arthur class no. 30765 *Sir Gareth* pictured in the yard at Eastleigh awaiting attention. This was another of the batch introduced in 1925 for the eastern section. It ended its days at Basingstoke, from where it was withdrawn in September 1962.   9.11.55

Dover shed, with King Arthur class no. 30776 *Sir Galagars* and N class 2–6–0 no. 31819. In the 1950s Dover had an allocation of nearly seventy locomotives, a considerable number of which were tank engines used on local branches. The depot closed in 1961.

3.7.53

When I visited Tonbridge two Stewarts Lane King Arthur class engines were under repair in the shed yard, both with cylinder problems. Here is no. 30768 *Sir Balin*, with a 'Not to be Moved' sign projecting from the buffer beam. With two of its most powerful engines out of action at the same time, doubtless there were a few problems at Stewarts Lane.

1.7.53

King Arthur class no. 30785 *Sir Mador de la Porte* runs light engine through Eastleigh station. This engine was allocated to 71A Eastleigh and was one of the batch originally built for the eastern section.   9.11.55

The King Arthur class engines looked very different when they were fitted with multiple-jet blastpipes and larger chimneys. No. 30755 *The Red Knight*, a Nine Elms engine at the time, is seen here at Eastleigh, where it was built and completed in March 1923. It received the Lemaitre blastpipes and chimney in March 1940. Withdrawal came in May 1957 from Basingstoke shed. It was cut up at Eastleigh the same month.   9.11.55

The seven members of the Remembrance N15X class were rebuilds of LBSCR 4–6–4Ts introduced in 1914. Maunsell commenced the rebuilding of these engines in 1934, and all were named. They were all allocated to Basingstoke depot, working services into Waterloo. No. 32328 *Hackworth* was photographed at Nine Elms as it arrived for servicing. 5.7.51

H15 class no. 30331 at Eastleigh shed. This engine was a 1924 rebuild of an F13 four-cylinder 4–6–0, a type first introduced in 1905. No. 30331 was a Salisbury engine and remained in service until March 1961. 8.11.55

Several of the H15 class 4–6–0s were allocated to Nine Elms in the early 1950s, no. 30484 among them. The H15s were a Urie design introduced by the LSWR in 1914. The first of the class to be withdrawn went in 1955, with the last going in 1961.   5.7.51

The driver of H15 class no. 30485 stands back as the fireman breaks up clinker at Nine Elms. This engine was the first of its class to be withdrawn, in April 1955. At this time members of the class could still be seen on express duties, especially at weekends or when there were motive power shortages. Withdrawals increased in 1959, with the last eight going in 1961.   12.7.54

Robert Urie was the Locomotive Superintendent of the London & South Western Railway from 1912 to 1922. During this time he introduced a number of highly respected designs, including the well-known N15 King Arthur class. His S15 class, designed for goods workings, was based on the N15. No. 30506, seen here at Feltham, was built in 1920 and remained in service until January 1964.   12.7.54

The K class 2–6–0s were introduced by the LBSCR in 1913, just prior to the outbreak of the First World War. Seventeen were built over an eight-year period; all were taken into British Railway stock and were withdrawn in 1962. No. 32344 is seen here taking coal at Three Bridges depot.   25.6.55

The interior of Ashford works, with a number of locomotives undergoing general overhaul or intermediate repairs. On the left are a number of tank engines undergoing overhaul. On the right is K class 2–6–0 no. 32353, and beyond it is L1 4–4–0 no. 31761. Numerous locomotive parts are to be seen in this picture. 1.7.53

(*Opposite*): The driver of U class no. 31806 watches for the signal from the station staff that everything is ready for the train to depart from Eastleigh. In the background an M7 0–4–4T carries out station pilot duties. 9.11.55

A considerable amount of work had already been completed on U1 2–6–0 no. 31899 before it was moved outside into Ashford works yard. The U1s were a three-cylinder development of the U class.   1.7.53

(*Opposite, top*): The U class was introduced by Maunsell in 1928. No. 31637, seen here at Dover, was among those built with smaller splashers and detail alterations. Other locomotives of this design were rebuilds of SECR K (River) class 2–6–4Ts, which had made their debut in 1917. This was also a three-cylinder development, classified U1.   3.7.53

(*Opposite, bottom*): Among the engines fresh from general overhaul at Ashford works was U class no. 31628. These locomotives were designed to meet the need for motive power to work semi-fast and cross-country passenger trains. The 2–6–0 design was already in hand, the first engine being completed at Brighton in 1928. Already in service were the River class 2–6–4Ts. Several derailments were experienced with the Rivers, however, and these engines were subsequently rebuilt as U class.   14.5.55

The N class 2–6–0s were designed for mixed traffic duties. Fifty were constructed at Ashford works from parts supplied by Woolwich Arsenal, with boilers built by the North British Locomotive Company. No. 31853, seen here at Hither Green, was one of these engines. Smoke deflectors were fitted as the locomotives passed through works from 1933 onwards.   24.5.56

(*Opposite*): The first N class 2–6–0 was introduced in 1917, at a time when there was an important need for more powerful locomotives to handle the increasingly heavy loads. In the years following the First World War Woolwich Arsenal produced complete sets of parts for these engines, with the exception of the boilers, which were supplied by the North British Locomotive Company. The engines were assembled at Ashford works. No. 31852, seen here at Dover, was completed in March 1925.   3.7.53

Being very familiar with the famous Great Northern Atlantics, I was keen to photograph those engines widely known as the Brighton Atlantics (class H2), which were still actively engaged on Newhaven boat trains. Here, no. 32421 *South Foreland* stands ready for its next duty at Brighton shed. Only six examples were built, in 1911–12, as a superheated development of the H1 class. Time was running out for the H2s still in service in 1955, as four were withdrawn the following year. The last, no. 32424 *Beachy Head*, survived until 1958.   26.5.55

Tucked away in an obscure corner of Brighton shed, H2 class no. 32424 *Beachy Head* was in a very difficult position for photography. The last Brighton Atlantic in service, it was withdrawn in 1958. These engines were very similar in appearance to the famous Great Northern C1 class.   25.6.55

In their final years the T9 class 4–4–0s were mostly to be found on local and cross-country services, passenger duties, parcels trains and empty stock workings. Here no. 30707 steams through Eastleigh station with a train that included two Pullman coaches and a miscellaneous collection of other stock. 9.11.55

T9 class no. 30310 waits at Eastleigh station at the head of a local train comprising three vintage coaches as a member of the station staff loads parcels into the front brake compartment. No. 30310 was an Eastleigh engine at this time. It later transferred to Bournemouth, from where it was withdrawn in May 1959, ending its days at Eastleigh works. 9.11.55

T9 4–4–0s were to be found at several Southern Region depots. No. 30338 is seen here inside Reading shed. This engine was built at Nine Elms works in October 1901 and completed just under sixty years' service.   7.8.55

The graceful lines of the T9 class 4–4–0s can be seen to good effect here as no. 30705 runs on shed at Nine Elms. This engine was built by Dubs & Co. and was completed in February 1899. Its final days were spent at Guildford shed, from where it was withdrawn in January 1958.   12.7.54

Eastleigh had a number of T9s in its allocation, including no. 30289, seen here in the spacious shed building. This engine was completed at Nine Elms works in February 1900 and withdrawn in November 1959, ending its days at Eastleigh works. 8.11.55

The T9 class 4–4–0s with their 6ft 7in driving wheels were capable of a fair turn of speed, which soon earned them the nickname 'Greyhounds'. They were one of Drummond's most successful designs. No. 30301 is seen here at Salisbury shed. This engine was one of ten that lost their eight-wheeled tenders in a complicated swap, receiving instead six-wheel tenders as seen here. 3.9.56

Surrounded by countless parts, Nine Elms T9 4–4–0 no. 30719 is seen minus wheels undergoing overhaul in Brighton works. At this time a number of T9s were allocated to the London depot. No. 30719 spent several years there before moving in June 1959 to Exmouth Junction, from where it was withdrawn in March 1961.   25.6.55

(*Opposite, top*): I was lucky to catch D15 class 4–4–0 no. 30467 standing in splendid isolation at Nine Elms depot. The D15s were principal express locomotives of their day and were popular with enginemen. This was the penultimate survivor of the class, being withdrawn in September 1955 after forty-three years' service. It was sent to Ashford works and cut up there.   12.7.54

(*Opposite, bottom*): Interested as I was in D1 4–4–0 no. 31741 and E4 no. 32565 at Bricklayers Arms, it was the engine behind the D1 that I really wanted to photograph. It was very frustrating as there was no way I could get a decent shot. It was B4X 4–4–0 no. 2045, one of the last of the class which became extinct in 1951. It had not received a BR number and its tender was still lettered 'Southern'.   1.11.51

The D1 and E1 rebuilds were introduced to handle continental expresses and other fast services, especially over the Chatham section where there were weight limitations. In due course many of these trains were taken over by King Arthurs. Rebuilding of these locomotives by Beyer, Peacock and Co. also took place at Ashford works. D1 no. 31727, seen here fresh from a general overhaul, was an Ashford rebuild, being completed in October 1922. It was withdrawn from Nine Elms in March 1961, the same year that the class became extinct.   14.5.55

(*Opposite, top*): The E1 4–4–0s were rebuilds of the E class. No. 31165, seen here undergoing a works overhaul at Ashford, was built in January 1908 and rebuilt as an E1 in May 1920. By coincidence, the last E class member, no. 31166, was at Ashford for scrapping at the same time.   14.5.55

(*Opposite, bottom*): The E class, one of the most graceful 4–4–0 designs to run on British Railways, was introduced by Wainwright for the SECR in 1905. No. 31166 of Faversham shed is seen here at Ashford. Built there in July 1907, it was the last of the class in service and was withdrawn in May 1955.   1.7.53

No. 31166 had reached the end of the line when this picture was taken, and it was awaiting scrapping at Ashford works. Built in July 1907, it was withdrawn in May 1955. During its last year in service it ran with a lined tender lettered 'British Railways', a replacement for its own which had become badly corroded. This engine almost reached one and a half million miles during its long working life.   14.5.55

Twenty-six E class 4–4–0s were built between 1906 and 1908, all at Ashford works. Eleven were rebuilt to become class E1 between 1919 and 1920. No. 31315, seen here at Bricklayers Arms shed, London, was running with its tender lettered 'British Railways'. This locomotive was withdrawn in March 1954.
                                                                                                              1.11.51

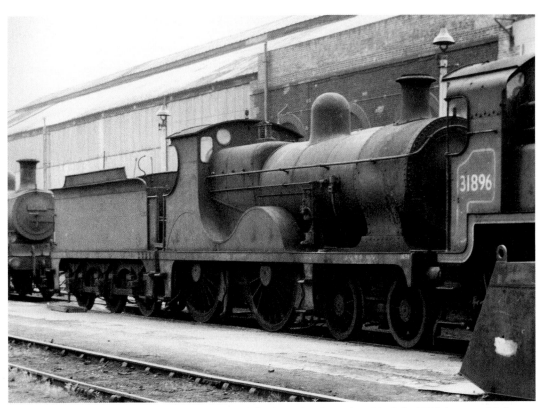

The end of the road for E class no. S1491 at Ashford works. Completed in July 1907, it was withdrawn in February 1953. This locomotive had been repaired at Ashford in 1948, receiving the S prefix which it carried through to withdrawal.   1.7.53

The 'Pride of Ashford', D class no. 31574 was kept in good external condition. The Ds were principal express locomotives of their day, but by the mid-1950s they had been relegated to secondary services. Fifty-one were built, of which twenty-one were rebuilt as D1 class. All of the un-rebuilt engines passed into British Railways stock. No. 31574 was withdrawn in October 1956.   14.5.55

D class no. 31750 was one of five built by the Vulcan Foundry, being completed in October 1903. Four private companies and Ashford works built the Ds. This engine was withdrawn in February 1953 from Reading depot and is seen here at Ashford works awaiting scrapping. 1.7.53

(*Opposite*): Ashford depot certainly kept D class 4–4–0 no. 31574 in excellent external condition. The Ds were widely known as 'Coppertops', a nickname that doubtless arose from their copper-capped chimneys and polished brass in SECR days. No. 31574 was completed at Ashford in February 1907 and remained in service until October 1956. 1.7.53

My first visit to Nine Elms will always remain in my memory thanks to the wide range of motive power I found there. The ex-SECR D class 4–4–0 no. 31075 was a Reading engine. It was built by Dubs & Co. in 1903 and completed just a month short of fifty years' service. On the right is an H class 0–4–4T and on the left Lord Nelson class no. 30860 *Lord Hawke*.   5.7.51

On my first visit to Nine Elms depot I was fortunate to find this veteran 4–4–0 standing in the yard. L11 class no. 30163 was built at Nine Elms works and completed in September 1903. Many of this forty-strong class had already been withdrawn and time was rapidly running out for no. 30163. Just three months later it was condemned, one of the twenty-two that went that year.   5.7.51

Scenes such as this were by no means uncommon, as the lack of space at some depots meant that repairs were often done outside. L class no. 31760, sporting the usual 'Not to be Moved' sign, is receiving attention from the fitters at Tonbridge. This engine was the first of the class to be built, being completed by Beyer, Peacock and Co. in August 1914.   1.7.53

In the 1950s numerous excursions and specials ran to seaside resorts. Here, L class no. 31763 stands outside Brighton station carrying a reporting number that indicates it worked in with a special. No. 31763 was a Tonbridge engine, and it remained there for several years. In June 1959 it moved to Nine Elms, from where it was withdrawn in April 1960.   25.6.55

Locomotives of the 4–4–0 wheel arrangement were to be found working local passenger services on most regions during the early 1950s. Here L class no. 31765 approaches Folkestone Central.   28.6.53

Tonbridge shed had a number of L class 4–4–0s in its allocation, including no. 31773. This engine was one of the batch built by A. Borsig of Tegel, Berlin. They arrived in Britain via Dover in a partially dismantled state and were prepared for service at Ashford works. No. 31773 was withdrawn in August 1959.   1.7.53

The L class was introduced in 1914 and twenty-two were built, twelve by Beyer, Peacock and Co. and ten by A. Borsig of Tegel, Berlin. All were delivered in 1914. No. 31776, pictured at Ashford shed, was one of those built by Borsig. It entered service in June 1914 and was withdrawn in February 1961 from Nine Elms.   1.7.53

During the 1950s the L class 4–4–0s were mostly to be seen on semi-fast and local passenger services. In the mid-1950s no. 31776 was allocated with two others to Brighton depot, working with other locomotives on the Tonbridge services before being transferred to Nine Elms in June 1959.   1.7.53

The branch engine on the Kent & East Sussex line's Headcorn to Rolvenden section was responsible for both passenger and goods traffic. Here 01 no. 31048 heads a goods train at Headcorn. This particular locomotive was the only one of its class with 5ft 1in driving wheels, compared with the 5ft 2in wheels of the other seven.   4.7.53

(*Opposite, top*): Four 01 class engines were allocated to Ashford in the mid-1950s and they were employed on light shunting duties locally, on the Kent & East Sussex line and on shunting in the works yard. No. 31064 was in good external condition when I photographed it on shunting work. It was withdrawn in May 1958 from Ashford and cut up the same month.   1.7.53

(*Opposite, bottom*): 01 class no. 31065 busy moving locomotives in the yard at Ashford works. This was the last survivor of the class, being withdrawn in June 1961 from Dover. These engines were instantly recognisable by their external frames and springs on the tender.   3.7.53

The eight surviving examples of the 01 class were allocated to Ashford and Dover depots during the 1950s. This is no. 31258 on shunting work at Dover. This engine was the penultimate survivor, being withdrawn from Dover in February 1961.　　　　　　　　　　　　　　　　　3.7.53

Typical of so many 0–6–0 tender locomotives of the period, this is 0395 class no. 30568 at Feltham depot. This engine was built by Neilson & Co. in 1883 and remained in service for a truly remarkable seventy-five years. At the time this picture was taken, locomotives of this class were to be seen on shunting duties at several south London locations.　　　　　　　　　　　　　　12.7.54

The Adams 0395 class, introduced in 1881, consisted of just eighteen survivors at nationalisation in 1948. A considerable number had been built, and fifty were sold to the War Department for service in the Middle East during the First World War. No. 30573, seen here at Feltham, was built by Neilson & Co. in 1883; it was withdrawn in November 1956.   12.7.54

The thirty examples of the LSWR 700 class 0–6–0s were all built by Dubs & Co. in 1897. All survived to be taken into British Railways stock. The first member of the class to be withdrawn went in 1957 as a result of collision damage, and another followed in 1959. Withdrawals were rapid during 1961 and in December 1962 the last was withdrawn. No. 30700 is seen here at Nine Elms.   5.7.51

Those members of the C2X class that were fitted with two domes presented an unusual appearance. These engines at one stage had two top feeds; this was later changed to one but the dome remained. No. 32438 was photographed at Brighton on a rather grey day.   26.6.55

The double-domed C2X class engines were known as 'Vulcans' because they were all constructed by the Vulcan Foundry. No. 32551 is seen here at Ashford following a general overhaul, ready to return to its home depot, Bricklayers Arms.   14.5.55

Fresh from a general overhaul, this is C class 0–6–0 no. 31691 in immaculate condition at Stewarts Lane depot. This particular engine was the first of the fifteen-strong batch built by Neilson Reid in 1900. It remained in service until withdrawn from Gillingham in February 1959, ending its days at Ashford works.   1.11.51

In the 1950s it was by no means uncommon to find locomotives under repair being moved out into the shed yard until work could be completed. This was the case with C class 0–6–0 no. 31277, which had had its middle set of driving wheels removed and was standing in the yard at Ashford. The engine had just three months' service left before being condemned.   14.5.55

One of the most useful wheel arrangements on all regions of British Railways was the 0–6–0 tender engine. There were several designs to be found on the Southern Region, with the robust C class being among the most numerous. They were introduced in 1900, and the majority were built at Ashford, with others completed at Longhedge and by two private contractors. No. 31498 is seen here at Ashford shed.   14.5.55

(*Opposite*): Another engine under repair at Tonbridge shed was C class no. 31272. This locomotive was built at Ashford in 1904 and withdrawn in August 1959. The C class 0–6–0s were to be found at most of the south-eastern section sheds. In the background is one of the easily recognisable Q class 0-6-0s introduced by Oliver Bulleid in 1942
1.7.53

In all, 109 C class 0–6–0s were built between 1900 and 1908, and all except two passed into British Railways ownership. One example had been rebuilt as an 0–6–0ST in 1917 and classified S class; it was withdrawn in 1951. No. 31510, seen here, was photographed at Hither Green.   24.5.56

(*Opposite, top*): The C class 0–6–0s were used on many duties during the 1950s. Here no. 31590 waits at Headcorn with a pick-up goods. This engine was allocated to Tonbridge, presumably the destination of the lightweight goods train, which no doubt would have picked up additional wagons en route.   4.7.53

(*Opposite, bottom*): The final Maunsell design was the Q class 0–6–0, which was intended for use on secondary routes working both goods and passenger services. Twenty were built, all at Eastleigh works. Steaming was improved on those fitted with multiple-jet blastpipes and larger squat chimneys. No. 30536, seen here at Eastleigh, was completed in October 1938. The equipment fitted above the middle set of driving wheels is a steam reverse. This engine was withdrawn in January 1964. In the background is King Arthur class no. 30784 *Sir Nerovens*.   8.11.55

The introduction of the Q1 Austerity class by O.V. Bulleid in 1942 aroused much comment. Forty of these piston-valve locomotives were built and were numbered between 33001 and 33040. No. 33019 is seen here at Ashford shed.   1.7.53

(*Opposite, top*): Although officially withdrawn in January 1966, Q1 no. 33006 was still at work at Eastleigh works. When this picture was taken the locomotive was in remarkably good external condition, having recently worked a rail tour. These were powerful engines with a tractive effort of 30,000lbs.   26.3.66

(*Opposite, bottom*): During most of the 1950s the Somerset & Dorset was under Southern Region control, changing to Western Region in 1958 and remaining there until it finished with steam in 1966. Bath (Green Park) was the principal shed, where this picture of S&D 2–8–0 no. 53810 was taken, carrying the 71G shedplate. Derby works still maintained these engines and the others used on the line.   31.8.55

Standard class 5 no. 73111 *King Uther* in the condition typical of the early 1960s pulls away from Clapham Junction with a train of parcels stock. This engine was to remain in service until 1965.   9.61

Chapter Two
Tank Engine Designs

Of the six regions of British Railways the Southern certainly had one of the greatest ranges of tank locomotive designs still in service in the 1950s. Pride of place had to be given to the three Beattie 2–4–0 'well tanks' working the Wenford Bridge mineral line, which had long outlived their classmates. The difficulties imposed by the branch resulted in their long working lives, although they had to be rebuilt several times over the years. In 1956 I planned a trip to the West Country. High on my list was a visit to Wadebridge, where the small depot looked after these Beattie 'well tanks'. I travelled to the various destinations by rail and I well recall arriving at Wadebridge on a dry but very overcast day to find no. 30586 in the yard with no. 30587 as spare engine in the small shed building. Where was no. 30585? In due course it returned from working on the branch, but unfortunately as it arrived so did torrential rain. However, there was no way I was going to miss taking a shot of this engine despite the weather, as it was impossible for me to return the next day.

My trip had commenced at Waterloo with a good run to Salisbury behind rebuilt Merchant Navy no. 35020 *Bibby Line* and a visit to Salisbury depot. Fortunately the Southern Region was one of those that would grant permits to individuals. I then went back to the station to catch a train to Axminster, where my objective was to photograph at least one of the 'elegant' Lyme Regis 4–4–2 tanks. Here again they had long outlived their classmates because they were so ideally suited to the restricted and difficult line between Axminster and Lyme Regis. Two engines worked the service until heavy overhauls were required for both, which resulted in a third locomotive being purchased in an extremely derelict condition from the East Kent Railway, to which it had been sold many years previously. After a full overhaul the third engine emerged ready for work, thus enabling its classmates to visit Eastleigh for general overhauls.

Fortunately, not long after I arrived at Axminster no. 30582 returned with the branch train, and I was later able to travel over the line on the last return service of the day. My next call was Exmouth Junction depot, the large shed that maintained the Lyme Regis tanks. Standing adjacent to the shed was Z class 0–8–0T no. 30950. The Z class engines were powerful and by the mid-1950s work was becoming short for them. After some difficulty they were allowed to work as bankers between Exeter Central and St David's stations, duties that were previously performed by E1R class 0–6–2 tanks. Fortunately for me, one of the latter was on shed pilot duty in the shed yard.

The Southern Region had many other interesting tank locomotives to be found at numerous locations. One of these was the Folkestone Harbour branch worked by R1 class 0–6–0Ts. Working trains down was no problem, but getting back up to the main line was a very different matter owing to the incline. Heavy boat trains required as many as three R1s at the front, with a fourth banking. As can be imagined, these made a very fine sight – and sound – as they crossed the swing bridge just after starting out. In addition, four members of the class in service in the early 1950s looked very different as they had been modified for use on the Whitstable branch. The fitting of a short Urie-type chimney considerably altered their appearance, but if they had the Stirling-type cab this was retained or refitted. One or two of these engines were to be found at Ashford shed transferring locomotives to and from the works, or on shed pilot duties.

Anyone interested in Southern steam dreamed of visiting Feltham depot, which was home to two very different tank locomotive classes. The four massive G16 class 4–8–0Ts were built for 'hump shunting' work, while the five H16 4–6–2Ts were designed for heavy freight traffic. Both types were introduced by the London & South Western Railway in 1921. Work was already becoming scarce for them in the mid-1950s, with one of the G16s dumped at the end of an isolated siding at the time of my visit. Judging by its appearance, it had not worked for some considerable time.

One place you could be sure of finding the Maunsell W class 2–6–4Ts was at Hither Green, as several were allocated to this depot. They were principally used on inter-regional freights and other local work. These engines were an attractive design developed from the N1 class 2–6–0s. Hither Green was a spacious depot, ideal for photography, unlike some which, apart from being smoky and cramped, were cluttered with a large number of posts and poles. Railway photography also relied on another very important factor – the weather. Bright clear conditions were perfect, but it was all very frustrating when it was dull, grey and raining, especially if you had travelled a considerable distance and had to obtain all various permits in the process. There was only one realistic option: if what you wanted was there, you had to make the best of the conditions and photograph it anyway, as you might not have another chance. The results were not always very good – but many such pictures show scenes that can now never be repeated and locomotives that will never be seen again.

The Lyme Regis branch engine also acted, when required, as station pilot at Axminster. No. 30582 is seen here prior to working the last branch line service of the day. The three surviving 4–4–2Ts, all built by different companies, were allocated to Exmouth Junction shed. These engines long survived their classmates, the last of which was scrapped in 1928. Despite trials of several other classes, until the early 1960s the 'radial tanks' were in absolute charge of the branch services. Following extensive work, Ivatt 2–6–2Ts took over.   3.9.56

Having completed another run, no. 30582 has arrived back at Axminster and is shortly to be released from the train to 'run round'. This engine was built by R. Stephenson & Co. and was completed in September 1885. It was withdrawn in July 1961, and in its amazing seventy-six years' service it covered more than two million miles. 3.9.56

No. 30582 again, heading the two-coach branch train at Lyme Regis ready to work the last train back to Axminster. The large spacious cab fitted to these elegant engines can be clearly seen, also the sizeable coal bunker. During the 1950s the Lyme Regis branch attracted enthusiasts from far and wide. 3.9.56

High on my list of places to visit in the 1950s was Wadebridge, home of the three veteran 2–4–0WTs, all of which I managed to photograph during my short stay. This is no. 30586 engaged on shunting. This engine was different from its two sisters as it had rectangular splashers.   5.9.56

(*Opposite, top*): On the day of my visit the weather was, to say the least, changeable. By the time no. 30585 arrived on shed the heavens had opened, and the driving rain is all too evident in this picture of the engine alongside the coaling shed. As I had to move on, there was nothing for it but to get wet! Note the curved splashers, also fitted to no. 30587.   5.9.56

(*Opposite, bottom*): The third of the Beattie 2–4–0WTs No. 30587 was out of use in the small shed in company with O2 class no. 30200. It was quite light in the building so I was able to get this picture. These three engines were the sole survivors of a class which became extinct in 1928. They were rebuilt on several occasions and remained in service on the Wenford Bridge mineral line until the 1960s.   5.9.56

The shunter hurries to uncouple the wagons as C14 no. 30588 carries out shunting work. Three C14s were still in work in the 1950s, one of them in departmental service. These engines were rebuilds of 2–2–0T railmotor trains, introduced in 1906.
9.11.55

(*Opposite, top*): One of the two Eastleigh depot C14 0–4–0Ts was used for shunting at Southampton West Quay. Here no. 30588 is seen running light on a very wet and windy November morning.
9.11.55

(*Opposite, bottom*): Two of these C14 class 0–4–0Ts, including no. 30589, were allocated to Eastleigh, one normally working at Southampton Town Quay, the other spare at the depot. Handrails and steps had been fitted to the front for use by the shunters. This engine was running with a B4 chimney and had lost its toolbox.
8.11.55

For many years the B4 class 0–4–0Ts were the principal shunting locomotives employed at Southampton Docks, although other members of the class were to be found at several depots. The Southampton Docks engines were all named, but no. 30094 was not one of these. This picture was taken at Plymouth Friary depot. The rather tattered remains of a spark arrestor can still be seen.

5.9.56

(*Opposite*): Another picture of no. 30589 at Eastleigh showing clearly the rather ungainly appearance of these engines. It was withdrawn in June 1957, with its sister engine no. 30588 being condemned six months later, leaving just 77S of the Engineer's Department to soldier on until April 1959.

8.11.55

Plymouth Friary depot was not large, having an allocation of just twenty-one engines in the mid-1950s, five of these being B4 class 0–4–0Ts. The only modern locomotives to be found there were four West Country lightweight Pacifics and an LMS-design 2MT 2–6–2T tank. Here no. 30094 stands ready for its next duty on the docks; it was withdrawn from service in 1957.   5.9.56

(*Opposite, top*): Thirty-four of the G6 class 0–6–0Ts were built at Nine Elms works between 1894 and 1900, and a considerable number of them were withdrawn shortly after nationalisation. No. 30162, seen shunting at Eastleigh, was completed in April 1900 and withdrawn in March 1958.   9.11.55

(*Opposite, bottom*): Two locomotive depots were in operation at Reading, one for the Western Region and the other for the Southern. At the time of my visit to the latter it was in the process of being run down, and in 1959 it became a sub-shed of Basingstoke. Two G6 0–6–0Ts were in its allocation, one of them being no. 30160. This engine was built at Nine Elms in 1900 and withdrawn in April 1959.   7.8.55

The famous Brighton works 'Terrier', resplendent in its LBSCR yellow livery, always attracted considerable attention as it carried out its shunting duties. This engine carried the Southern number 2635 until 1946, when it was transferred to service stock and became no. 377S. At this time it was painted bright yellow, a very welcome sight after the drab war years. In 1959 it returned to capital stock, becoming no. 32635. 14.7.54

(*Opposite*): Another view of no. 377S in its yellow LBSCR livery. Note the lining out on its buffer beam. 25.6.55

Having taken over the branch train at Rolvenden, Stroudley 'Terrier' no. 32655 stands ready to work the single-coach train to Robertsbridge Junction. This engine is one of the batch rebuilt with Marsh boiler and extended smokebox.   4.7.53

By 1953 there was very little passenger traffic on the Kent & East Sussex Railway, hence the single coach headed by 'Terrier' no. 32655. A guard's van has been attached, which was presumably dropped off at some point en route to Robertsbridge. There was very little room in the cab of the engine, so the bucket was hung on a bracket near the locomotive's toolbox.   4.7.53

Ashford works built just eight of these small P class 0–6–0Ts in 1909–10 and they were used as railmotors, often running with the engine between two driving coaches. Unfortunately, they were not very successful. No. 31556 is seen here as shed pilot at Brighton. Built in 1909, this engine spent some time during the First World War on shunting work at Boulogne for the Railway Operating Division. 14.7.54

One P class 0–6–0T was allocated to Eastleigh throughout most of the 1950s. On my visit I found no. 31178 standing in the yard dwarfed by larger locomotives. This engine was completed in February 1910 and withdrawn in June 1958, when it was sold to Messrs Bowaters at Ridham Dock. 9.11.55

Four of the Stirling R1 class 0–6–0Ts were fitted with Urie chimneys and cut-down mountings. The Stirling cab was retained or refitted as required. These locomotives were used on the long since gone Canterbury–Whitstable line. In the mid-1950s one of them was used to transfer engines requiring attention at Ashford works and also brought back the engines fresh from repair or general overhaul. No. 31147 is seen here at Ashford depot with locomotives ex-works. 14.5.55

(*Opposite, top*): In 1938 R1 no. 31010 was fitted with a Urie chimney but it retained the original Stirling-type cab in order to enable it to work on the Whitstable branch. It is seen here on shunting duties at Ashford depot. 1.7.53

(*Opposite, bottom*): I took this photograph as R1 no. 31107 and two sister engines were preparing to run down to the harbour station to collect a boat train and take it to the sidings at Folkestone Junction station, where a Bulleid Pacific would be waiting to commence its run to London Victoria. The sturdy R1s working in unison made a fine sight as they started out from Folkestone Harbour station with a heavy boat train. 3.7.53

The small shed at Folkestone Junction was a sub-depot of Dover. In the 1950s it had its own allocation, consisting of seven R1 class 0–6–0Ts that were used mainly on the Folkestone Harbour branch. Here one of them, no. 31047, stands outside the shed building. The depot was also used for servicing locomotives arriving with boat trains.   5.7.53

(*Opposite*): R1 no. 31154 pictured during a quiet moment at Folkestone Junction shed.   1.7.53

The R1 0–6–0Ts working the Folkestone Harbour branch were generally kept in good mechanical and external condition to cope with the comparatively short periods of very hard work hauling heavy boat trains up to the junction station. Thirteen R class 0–6–0Ts were rebuilt to R1 in the period 1910–22, and all were taken into British Railway stock, with the last being withdrawn in 1960. Here no. 31107 stands outside the shed awaiting its next duty. 3.7.53

(*Opposite, top*): The all-Pullman 'Golden Arrow' leaves the sidings at Folkestone Junction for the harbour station behind R1 no. 31340. One point of interest is the four-wheeled flat wagon which is carrying some type of containers. On the left-hand side of the picture is the connection from the main line to the harbour line siding. 5.7.53

(*Opposite, bottom*): The Folkestone Harbour branch certainly kept the R1 tanks busy. Here no. 31340 arrives with another connecting service. The boat trains nearly always had two luggage vans in their make-up, and in this case just one Pullman coach. 27.6.53

No fewer than four locomotives were required to work the heavy cross-channel boat trains from Folkestone Harbour to the junction station and the veteran R1 class 0–6–0Ts were employed on this work. The normal method was to have three locomotives at the front and a fourth banking. Here nos 31337, 31037 and 31047 start out on the climb . . .

. . . with no. 31107 banking.   8.7.53

R1 no. 31128 on pilot duties at Folkestone Central station. The majority of the R1s at Folkestone Junction depot were employed on the steeply graded harbour branch, which had weight restrictions.   8.7.53

R class no. 31661 0–4–4T in store at Folkestone Junction shed. This class was introduced by Kirtley for the London, Chatham & Dover Railway in 1891.   5.7.53

The last of the R class 0–4–4Ts was no. 31666, seen here at Tonbridge. During their long history, these engines were rebuilt with H-class boilers and many, including no. 31666, were also fitted for push-pull working.   1.7.53

(*Opposite, top*): Thirty-six of these D3 class 0–4–4Ts were built by the LBSCR to the design of L.B. Billinton between 1892 and 1896. By the mid-1950s very few remained in service. I was lucky to catch no. 32390 in the yard at Brighton as it was the last survivor. From the mid-1930s many were fitted for push-pull working, including no. 32390.   14.7.54

(*Opposite, bottom*): The E3 class was introduced by L.B. Billinton in 1894 for the LBSCR, and it was followed a few years later by the E4 design, which was a development having a Marsh boiler, larger wheels and extended smokebox. E3 no. 32167 was photographed at Brighton shed.   25.6.55

Shunting work at Southampton Docks was never-ending. Here E1 no. 32151 pulls away from one of the loading sheds with an assortment of wagons on a wet and windy day.   9.11.55

The shunter's pole, as demonstrated here by the shunter working with E1 no. 32113 at Southampton Docks, was once an everyday sight on British Railways. Four E1s were in use on the Isle of Wight during the 1950s, with just eight remaining on shunting work on the mainland.   9.11.55

Introduced in 1874, the E1 0–6–0Ts did not easily betray their age, largely thanks to their reboilering in Marsh days. No. 32606 is seen here shunting at Southampton Docks against a background of cranes.   9.11.55

E1 no. 32113 shunts Italian Railway wagons at Southampton Docks. Three E1 class locomotives were at work on the day of my visit, although two was the usual allocation at the Dock sheds. In total, seventy-nine E1s were built between 1874 and 1891. Ten were later rebuilt as 0–6–2Ts and classified E1R. The E1s had a long history. The first was withdrawn in 1908 and the last in 1961.   9.11.55

The E1 0–6–0Ts were introduced by Stroudley for the London, Brighton & South Coast Railway in 1874. During their long service they were all reboilered by Marsh during his period as Locomotive Superintendent of the Company (1905–11). No. 32606 was a regular Southampton Docks engine for several years.
9.11.55

The ten E1R 0–6–2Ts had a larger bunker and were designed for passenger services in the West Country. In the 1950s a number were to be seen at Exmouth Junction shed, where their duties included banking between Exeter Central and St David's until this work was taken over by the Z class 0–8–0Ts. No. 32697 was engaged on shunting when this picture was taken.
5.9.56

The E2 class consisted of ten 0–6–0Ts, introduced by the LBSCR in 1913 to the design of L.B. Billinton. The last five engines, introduced in 1915, had tanks extending further forward. No. 32107, seen here at Stewarts Lane, was one of the second batch. Although it had already received its British Railways number, the tank side was still lettered Southern and the old number is still visible.   1.11.54

It was by no means unusual to see locomotives still carrying the lettering 'Southern' in 1951, especially those of tank design. The new smokebox numberplate was in place on E4 no. 32493 at Nine Elms and the correct British Railway number was on the side of the bunker. In due course someone would no doubt have applied a British Railway crest to the tank sides.   5.7.51

Seventy-five E4 class 0–6–2Ts were built by the LBSCR between 1897 and 1903, and four were rebuilt to E4X in 1909–11. All except one passed into British Railways ownership. These engines were to be found at many depots, including Nine Elms, where this picture of no. 32497 was taken. They proved very useful engines and it was not until 1962 that the last examples made their final journey.   24.5.56

(*Opposite, top*): The E4 class was a development by L.B. Billinton of the earlier LBSCR E3 design, having larger wheels, a different boiler and an extended smokebox. These very useful engines were to be found at a number of depots on the Southern Region. No. 32563 is seen here at Eastleigh awaiting attention in the works.   9.11.55

(*Opposite, bottom*): E4 class no. 32556, fresh from general overhaul at Ashford works, stands at the running shed ready to return to its home depot, Eastleigh. Note the top disc bearing a 'special' sign.   1.7.53

E4 class no. 32579 under repair in Eastleigh shed, with a 'Not to be Moved' sign on the footplate. This engine was fitted to work push-pull services. In the background is M7 0–4–4T no. 30024, fresh from general overhaul.   8.11.55

(*Opposite*): By 1953 E5 class 0–6–2T no. 32593 was being used to supply steam at Dover shed. The buffers had been removed and the engine positioned hard against the buffer stop. The E5s were introduced to the London, Brighton & South Coast Railway in 1902 to the design of L.B. Billinton. In the background is N class no. 31852.   3.7.53

I was lucky to capture E6X no. 32407 at Ashford. Only two of the ten E6s were rebuilt as E6X; introduced in 1911, the modified engines had larger C3-type boilers and both were allocated to Norwood Junction depot in the early 1950s.   1.7.53

Locomotives built by two of the main constituent companies of the Southern Railway pictured at Nine Elms. H class 0–4–4T no. 31553 was a South Eastern & Chatham Railway design, while L11 no. 30163 originated from the London & South Western Railway.   5.7.51

H class 0–4–4T no. 31328 of Dover shed pictured at Minster. Judging by the amount of ash deposited on the track, it was by no means unusual for the fireman to clean the fire there. 6.7.53

Fresh from general overall at Ashford works and resplendent in lined livery, H class 0–4–4T no. 31306 of Gillingham shed waits for its return journey. Built at Ashford in 1906, this engine was fitted for push-pull working in November 1959. 1.7.53

Enginemen take the opportunity to have a chat at Ashford. H class 0–4–4T no. 31512 is showing a good head of steam, the fire having just been cleaned out. Note the large pile of ash and clinker. This engine was among those fitted for push-pull working. Note the large dents at the top of the Westinghouse pump. Presumably it had caused problems at some stage – such problems were normally rectified with a sharp blow from a coal hammer or spanner.   1.7.53

Coal had been piled high in the bunker of H class 0–4–4T no. 31320 at Brighton, and it's anyone's guess how much would have been lost when the engine moved off! This picture shows clearly the pipework required on engines fitted for push-pull working, and the Westinghouse pump on the front of the engine.   14.7.54

For a considerable time a single O2 class 0–4–4T, no. 30221, was allocated to Nine Elms, where it was mostly used on shed pilot duties. It was withdrawn from service in August 1953. 5.7.51

Two O2 class 0–4–4Ts, nos 16 and 24 *Ventnor* and *Calbourne* respectively, are seen here at Ryde Pier station, which would soon become busy with the arrival of the ferry from Portsmouth. When this picture was taken several of the Isle of Wight O2s had already been withdrawn owing to line closures. 11.9.59

This scene is typical of family holidays in the 1950s, when the majority of people still travelled by train. Little attention was paid to no. 21 *Sandown* as it travelled from Ryde Pier to Esplanade station with one of the island's rail services.   11.9.59

(*Opposite, top*): The O2 class 0–4–4Ts on the Isle of Wight were fitted with Westinghouse brakes and enlarged bunkers, and all were named. Here no. W16 *Ventnor* pulls away from Ryde Esplanade station. This engine was built at Nine Elms works in 1892.   11.9.59

(*Opposite, bottom*): The Adams O2 class 0–4–4Ts were best remembered for their work on the Isle of Wight, prior to electrification of the island's lines. There were, of course, others on the mainland, which were normally used on branch line services. No. 30179, seen here at Eastleigh, was based at Dorchester, a small shed with just seven engines in its allocation.   8.11.55

Wadebridge was a very small shed, with just five locomotives allocated to it. These consisted of the three Beattie 2–4–0WTs and a pair of O2s, including no. 30200, seen here inside the shed. Built at Nine Elms works in 1891, this engine had a long working life, being withdrawn in August 1962.   5.9.56

Members of the M7 class had a long association with the London area, where their duties included stock workings in and out of Waterloo, together with many other tasks. No. 30241, its tank sides still lettered 'British Railways', is pictured during a quiet moment at Waterloo.   5.7.51

M7 no. 30049, fresh from general overhaul at Eastleigh works, is prepared for the run back to its home depot, Horsham. This engine was fitted for working push-pull trains. Built in 1905, it remained in service until 1962.   8.11.55

In total, 105 examples of the M7 class 0–4–4Ts were built between 1897 and 1911, all of them at Nine Elms works except for ten that were constructed at Eastleigh. A considerable number were fitted for push-pull working, including no. 30125 seen here at Eastleigh. This engine was completed in August 1911 and remained in service until December 1962.   8.11.55

Engines were constantly being moved about at Eastleigh shed and push-pull-fitted M7 0–4–4T no. 30481 was engaged on this work at the time of my visit. In the early 1950s the depot had an allocation of over 140 engines, including eleven King Arthurs and eight Lord Nelsons. By the end of the decade these figures were nine and thirteen respectively.   9.11.55

Nine Elms M7 0–4–4T no. 30243, pictured after receiving intermediate repairs at Eastleigh works. It was customary to repaint the smokebox and chimney when work had been completed.   9.11.55

The M7 class 0–4–4Ts were built over a long period of time. The first was introduced in 1897, with the last being completed in December 1911. Many of these engines survived into the 1960s. No. 30323 was completed in October 1900 and withdrawn in December 1959. This picture was taken at Exmouth Junction, which had several M7s in its allocation.   5.9.56

The M7s were widely used on branch line trains in the west of England. No. 30667 is seen here at Exmouth Junction shed. As the principal work of these engines was passenger duties they carried lined-out livery. This engine was withdrawn in November 1960 and scrapped as no. 30106! There were a number of identity changes at this time.   5.9.56

In the early 1960s M7 class 0–4–4Ts were still employed on stock workings in the London area. No. 30035 is seen here on these duties at Clapham Junction. This engine completed sixty-five years in service, including some time in the West Country, and was withdrawn in February 1963.   9.61

M7 no. 30320 waits patiently at Clapham Junction for the signal to work empty stock for a Bournemouth train to Waterloo. All the M7s employed on these duties were withdrawn in February 1963 from Nine Elms shed.   9.61

The fact that I was keen to visit Hither Green shed was due in no small part to the W class 2–6–4Ts allocated there. Among these engines' duties were inter-regional freights. Introduced by Maunsell in 1931, they were a development of the N1 class 2–6–0s. Here no. 31913 stands outside the shed alongside King Arthur class no. 30772 *Sir Percivale*. 24.5.56

The depot at Hither Green was good for photography as it had plenty of space and was generally free of posts and poles. Here no. 31912 takes water before leaving the shed. Seven of the fifteen-strong W class 2–6–4Ts were allocated to Hither Green, being joined in the late 1950s by a further example. 24.5.56

W class 2–6–4T no. 31923 moves slowly away from the coaling plant at Hither Green shed. Engines of this class were used entirely on freight workings, largely because of previous problems with the unsuccessful River class 2–6–4Ts.   24.5.56

(*Opposite, top*): The massive proportions of the Z class 0–8–0Ts can be seen in this picture of no. 30950 at Exmouth Junction. This engine was the first of the class to be completed, in March 1929, and all eight were built at Brighton works. Despite its size, no. 30950 ran over half a million miles in its thirty-three years' service. The duties of the Exmouth Junction engines included banking between Exeter Central and St David's stations.   3.9.56

(*Opposite, bottom*): The powerful 0–8–0 Z class tank locomotives were built as yard shunters, but by the mid-1950s work for them was becoming scarce. No. 30951 had been moved to the end of an isolated siding at Three Bridges depot. Nevertheless, all eight remained in service until the end of 1962.   25.6.55

Judging by the rust on the wheels, G16 no. 30493 had not worked for a considerable time, having been 'put out to grass'. This engine was withdrawn in December 1959 and sent to Eastleigh works (where it was built in 1921) for scrapping.   12.7.54

(*Opposite*): One depot not to be missed in the 1950s was Feltham, which was home to the four massive G16 class 4–8–0Ts and the five H16 4–6–2Ts. Both were designed by Urie for the LSWR, the former for 'hump shunting' and the latter as heavy freight locomotives. H16 class 4–6–2T no. 30517 is seen here over the ash pits at Feltham. All five H16s were built at Eastleigh in 1921–2 and all were withdrawn in 1962.   12.7.64

This picture illustrates the massive size of the G16 class 4–8–0Ts. No. 30495 had just returned to Feltham and was about to have its fire cleaned over the ash pits. The long tool leaning against the engine was used to break up any clinker.   12.7.54

The four G16 class members were heavy tank locomotives weighing over 95 tons and principally designed for 'hump shunting' at Feltham marshalling yards. Other duties included local goods workings. Two of the class were withdrawn in 1959. No. 30495, seen here at Feltham, was withdrawn along with no. 30494 in December 1962, having done little work in the previous three years.   12.7.54

After the war several dumps of surplus motive power built up in various parts of the country, containing both British and American War Department locomotives. The Southern Railway purchased fourteen USA 0–6–0 tank engines to replace its B4 0–4–0Ts that were in need of major repairs. Southampton Docks had a small shed within the docks complex, where fourteen USA tanks and two E1 0–6–0Ts were allocated. The USA tanks, after some modification, proved ideal for working on the docks. Here no. 30072 stands in the shed yard awaiting its next duty. 9.11.55

The wet greasy rails resulted in USA tank no. 30063 having to work hard to start a heavy train for the Southampton 'Old docks', sending a plume of dense black smoke high in the air . . .

. . . before it finally got under way. Vulcan built this engine in 1942 and it entered service on the Southern Railway in October 1947. It completed fifteen years' service and was the first of the class to be withdrawn, in 1962.   9.11.55

The extensive rail system at Southampton Docks required a considerable number of locomotives to cover all the various shunting activities. No. 30067 is seen here moving vans on duty no. 3. Built by Vulcan in 1942, it entered service on the Southern Railway in May 1947. Withdrawn in July 1967, it was one of five stored at Salisbury awaiting disposal.   9.11.55

USA tank no. 30062 on dockyard shunting duties. The sturdy proportions of these powerful engines are clearly seen in this picture.   9.11.55

Gradually diesels began to take over the dockyard duties of the USA tank engines. No. 30071 is seen here at Eastleigh just a few months before steam finished on the Southern Region.   12.3.67

Six of the ex-US Army Transportation Corps 0–6–0Ts ended their working days in departmental service. Withdrawn no. DS 233 (formerly no. 30061) is seen here at Eastleigh, having been used at Redbridge sleeper depot from October 1962. This engine was the only one of the class built by Porter; the others were all constructed by Vulcan. 12. 3. 67

Ivatt 2MT 2–6–2Ts were allocated to a number of Southern Region depots. Having run into mechanical trouble, no. 41307 is seen here at Three Bridges awaiting the return of its pony truck. 25.6.55

In the 1950s Fairburn 2–6–4T 4MT tank locomotives were allocated to a number of Southern Region depots. Here no. 42070 of Ramsgate shed arrives at Margate with a local passenger service. Points of interest are the two water cranes and supply tanks seen in this picture.   6.7.53

The Fairburn 2–6–4Ts took over many of the local passenger services previously worked by elderly 4–4–0s. No. 42073, an Ashford engine, is seen here ready to leave Dover shed. The Fairburn 2–6–4Ts were a development of the well-tried Stanier design introduced in 1945.   3.7.53

Several Fairburn 2–6–4Ts were allocated to Ashford and Dover for working local passenger services. No. 42074 of Ashford depot is seen here heading a local service. In the background the brass carriage door handles are being polished.   1.7.53

The Standard class 3MT 2–6–2Ts were widely used on cross-country services. No. 82014 had just taken on water when this picture was taken at Eastleigh. This engine was one of four allocated to the depot at this time. Note the signal on the building on the right of this picture, and the long ladder required to reach the platform.   9.11.55

Large heaps of ash and clinker surround the area at Eastleigh where locomotives coming on shed had their fires cleaned. Standard 4MT no. 80016 was a Brighton engine. These locomotives made their debut in 1951 and soon proved to be both popular and powerful.   9.11.55

Having just been completed at Brighton works, Standard 4MT 2–6–4T no. 80088 was undergoing steaming tests before being handed over to the running department. Brighton built a considerable number of these locomotives.   14.7.54